Embracing our Features

Authored by Dashawn"BillBill" Johnson

ISBN: **978-1-7377923-3-8**

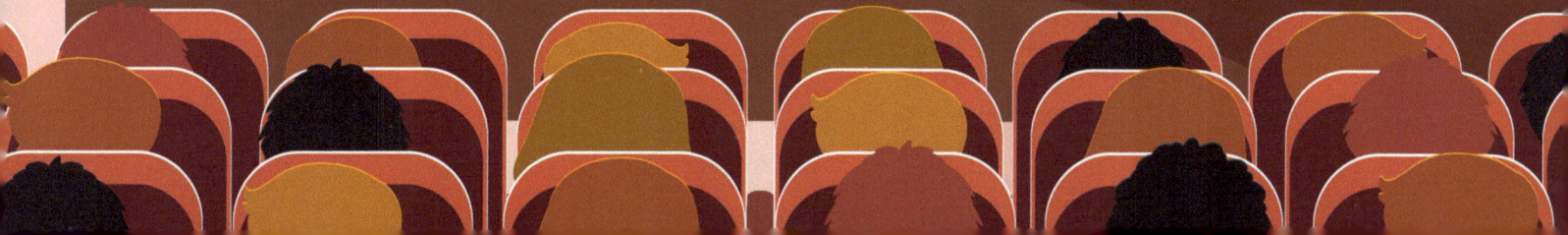

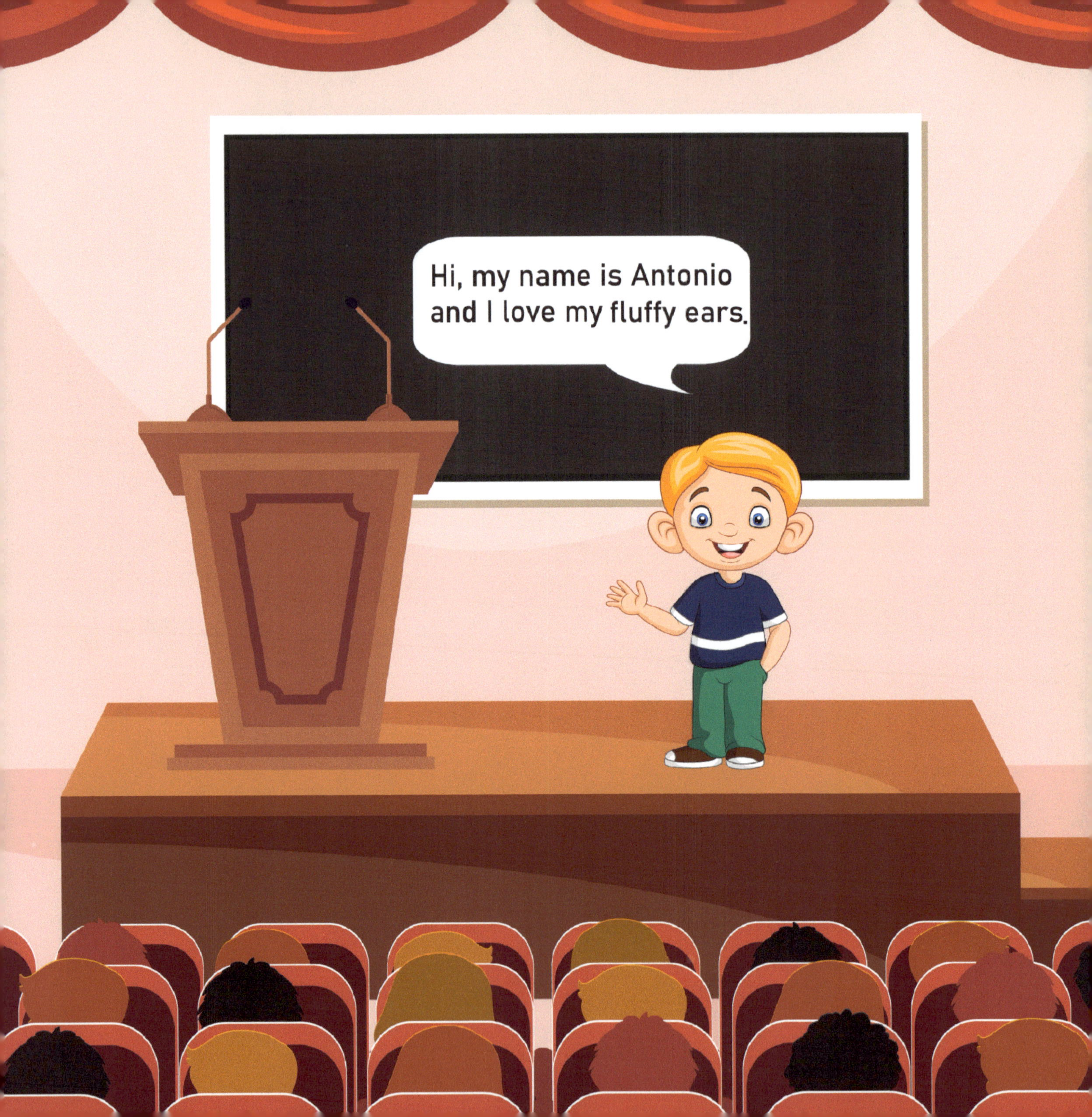
Hi, my name is Antonio
and I love my fluffy ears.

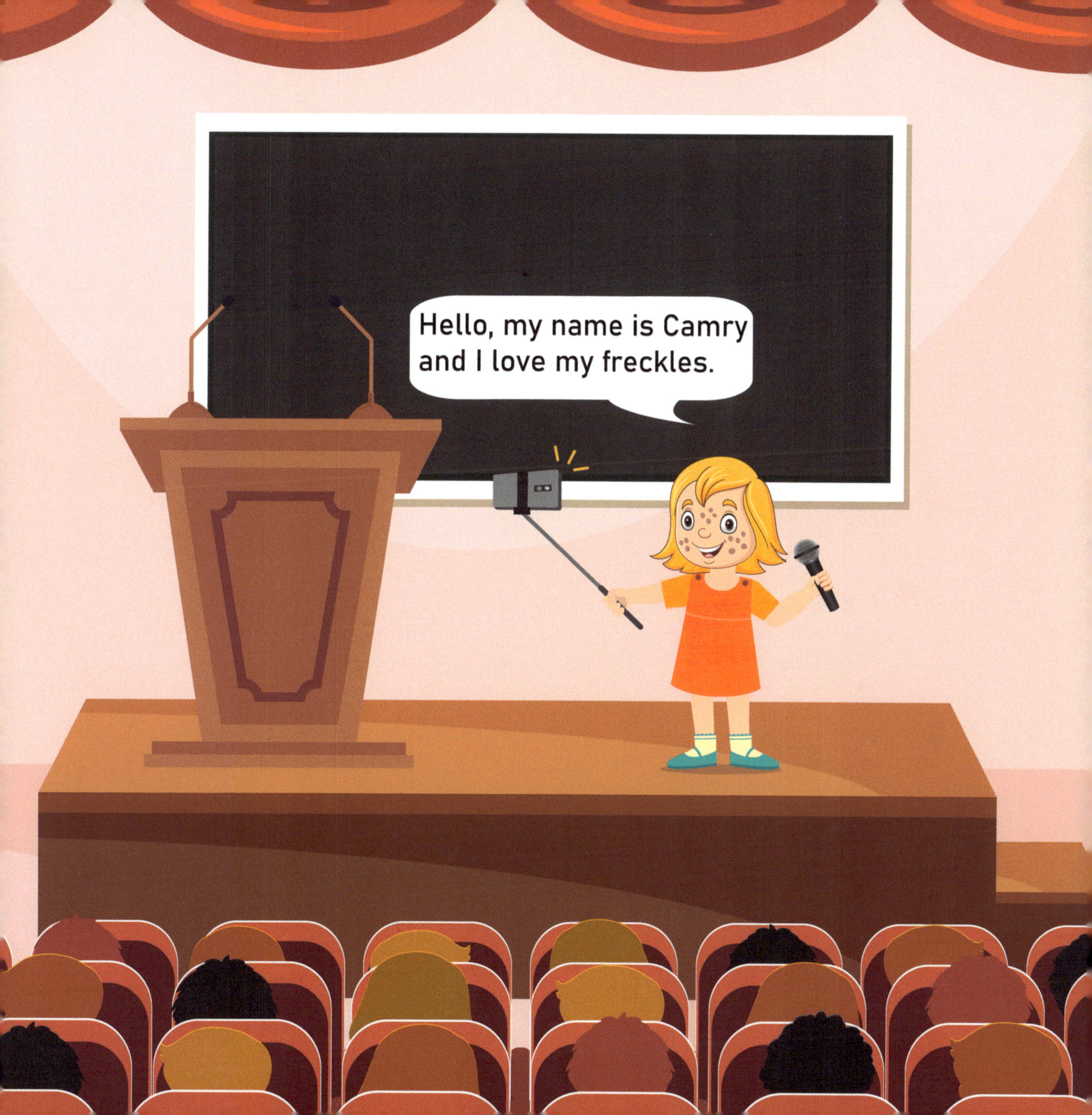
Hello, my name is Camry and I love my freckles.

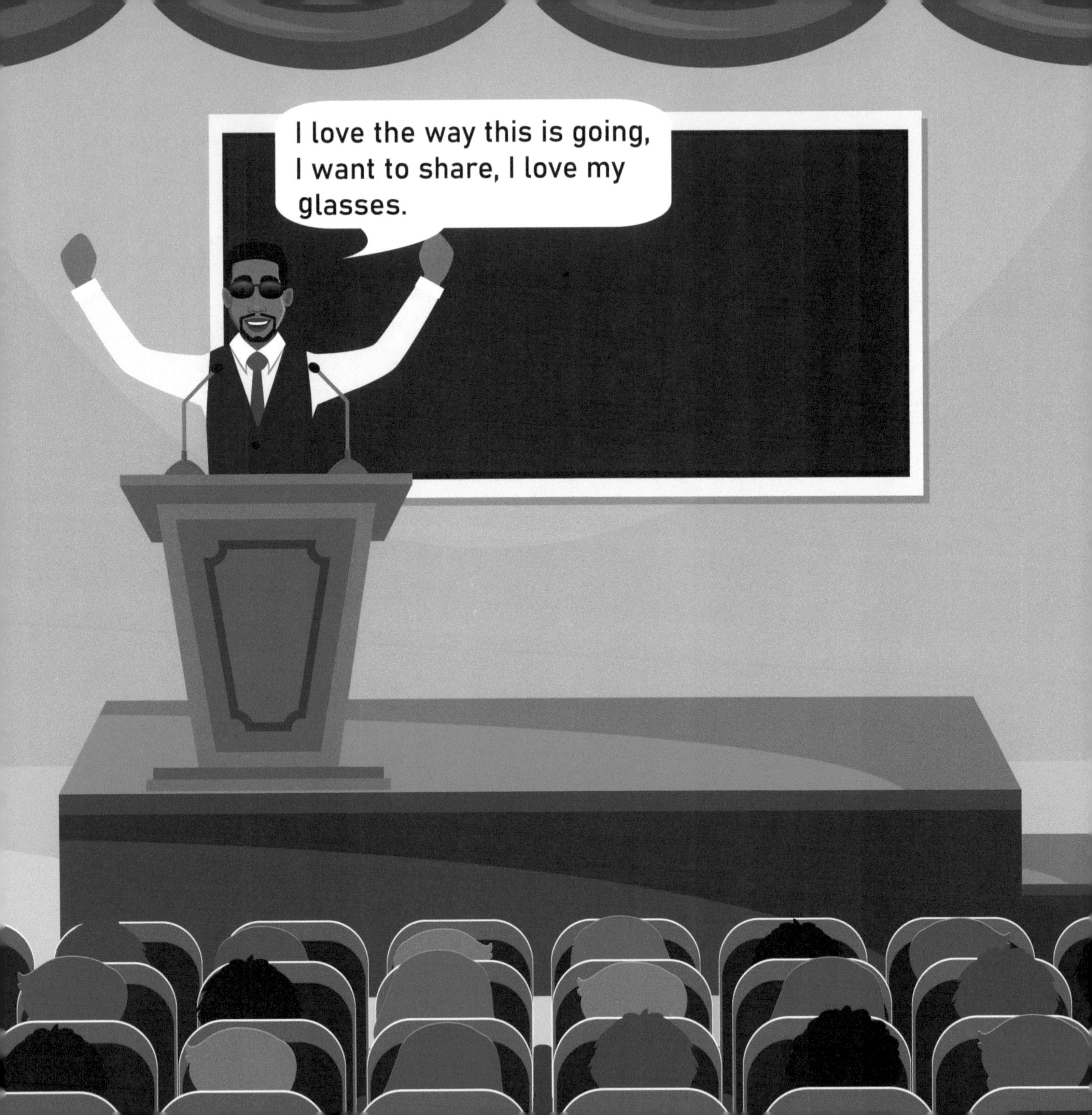
I love the way this is going, I want to share, I love my glasses.

Hello, y'all I'm Dashawn and I share my passion with Georgia.
Yes! We embrace our features.

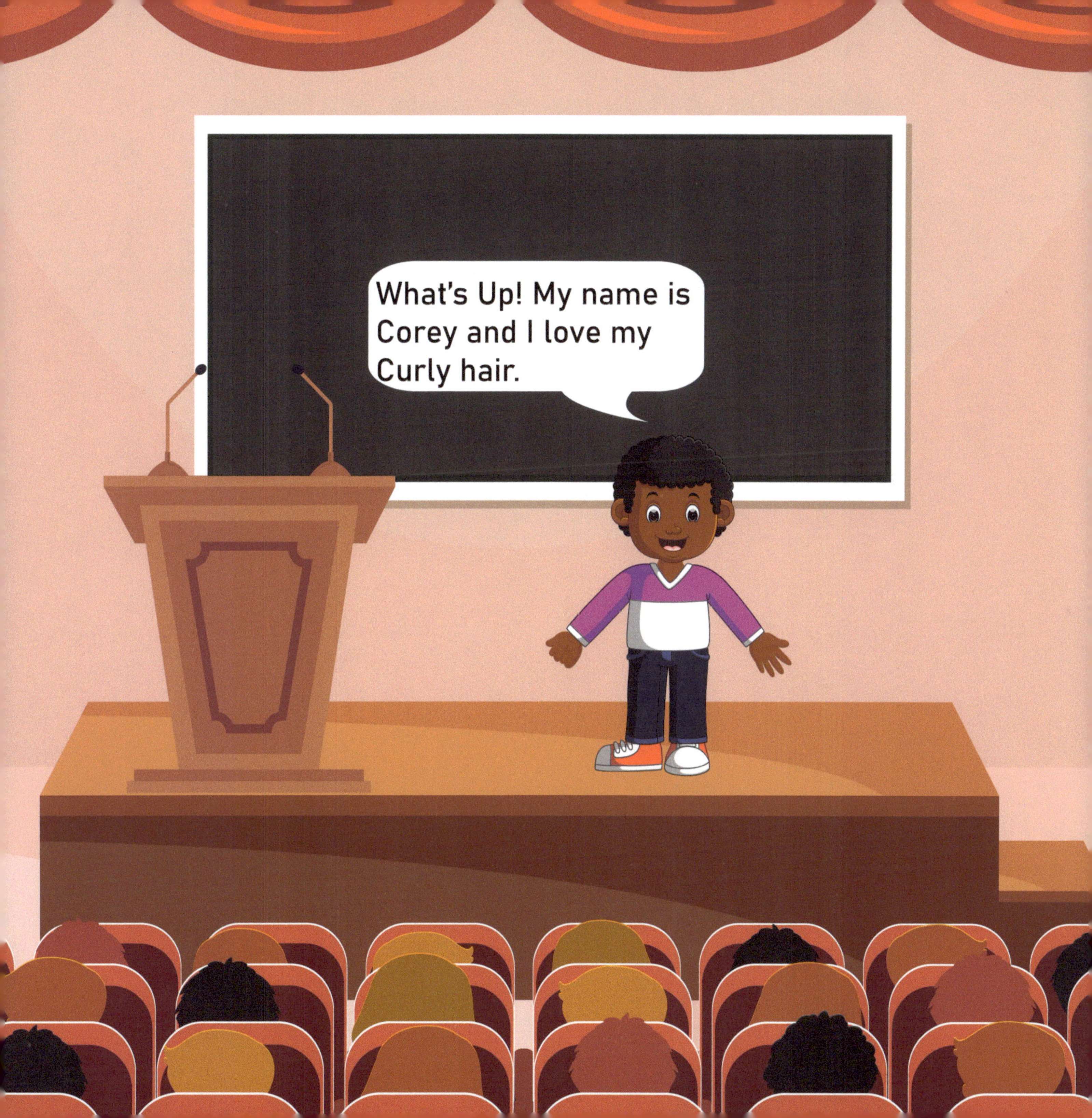
What's Up! My name is Corey and I love my Curly hair.

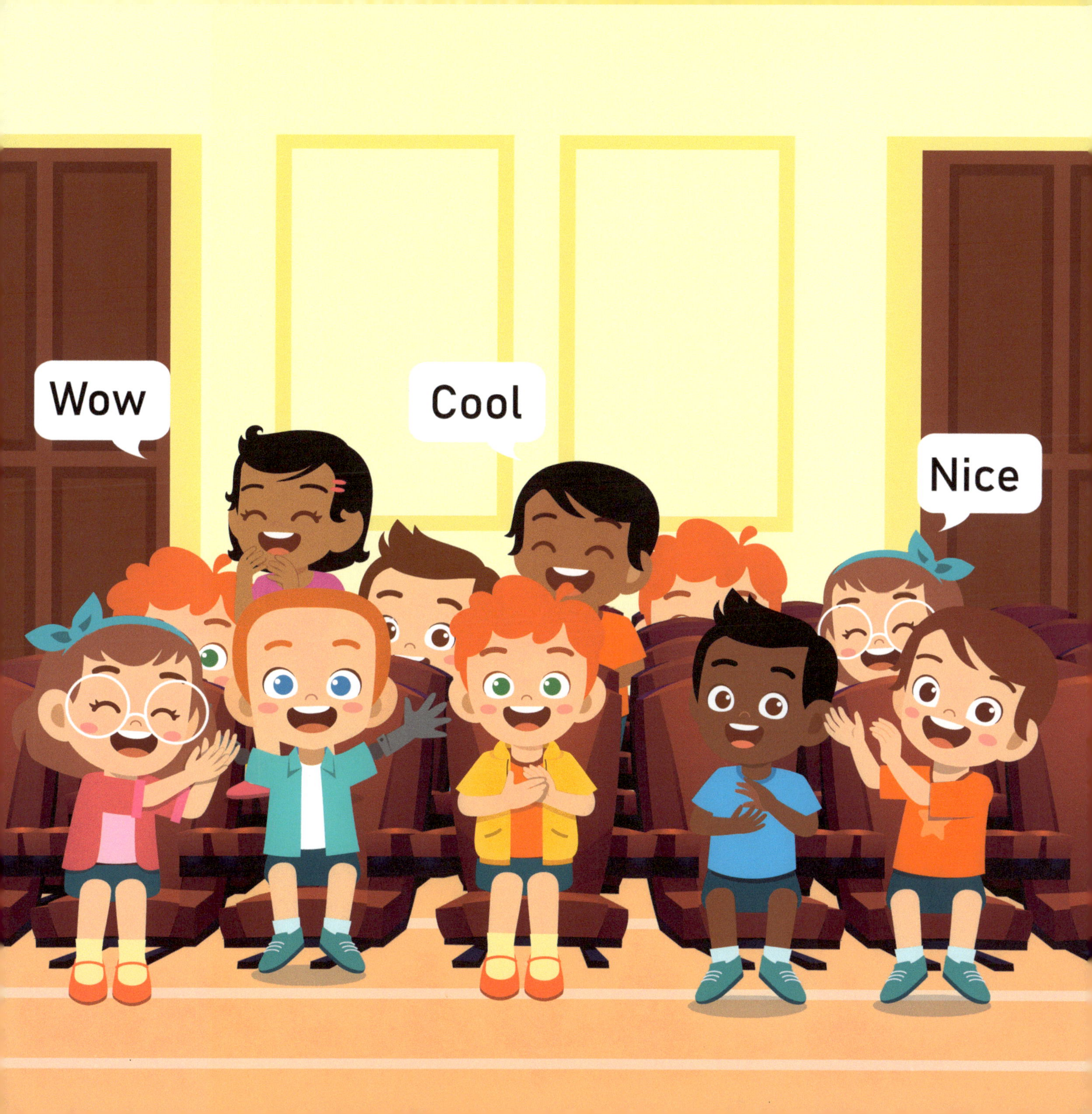
Wow
Cool
Nice

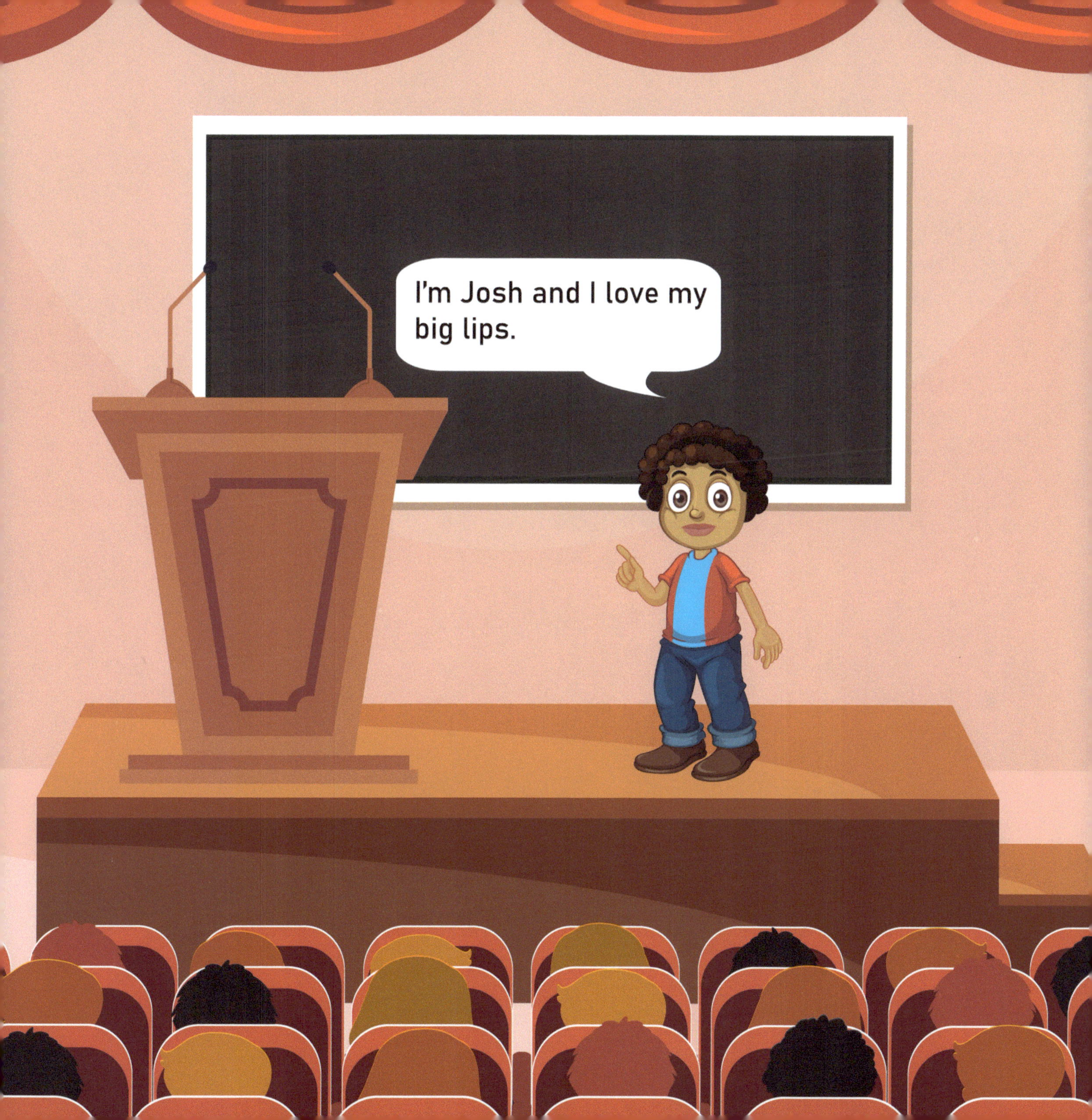
I'm Josh and I love my big lips.

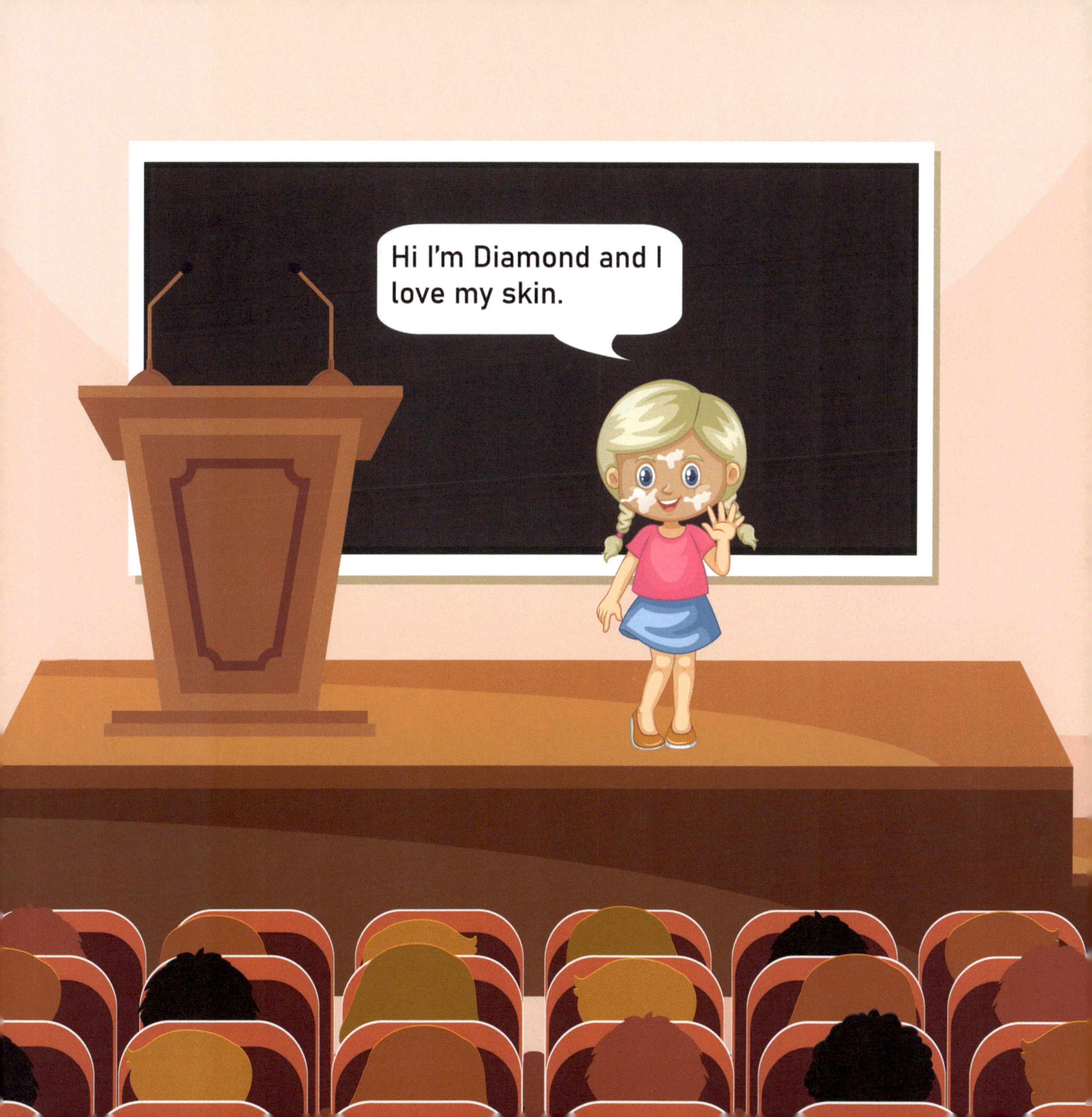
Hi I'm Diamond and I love my skin.

We love each other.
Color and gender doesn't matter.
We are best friends.

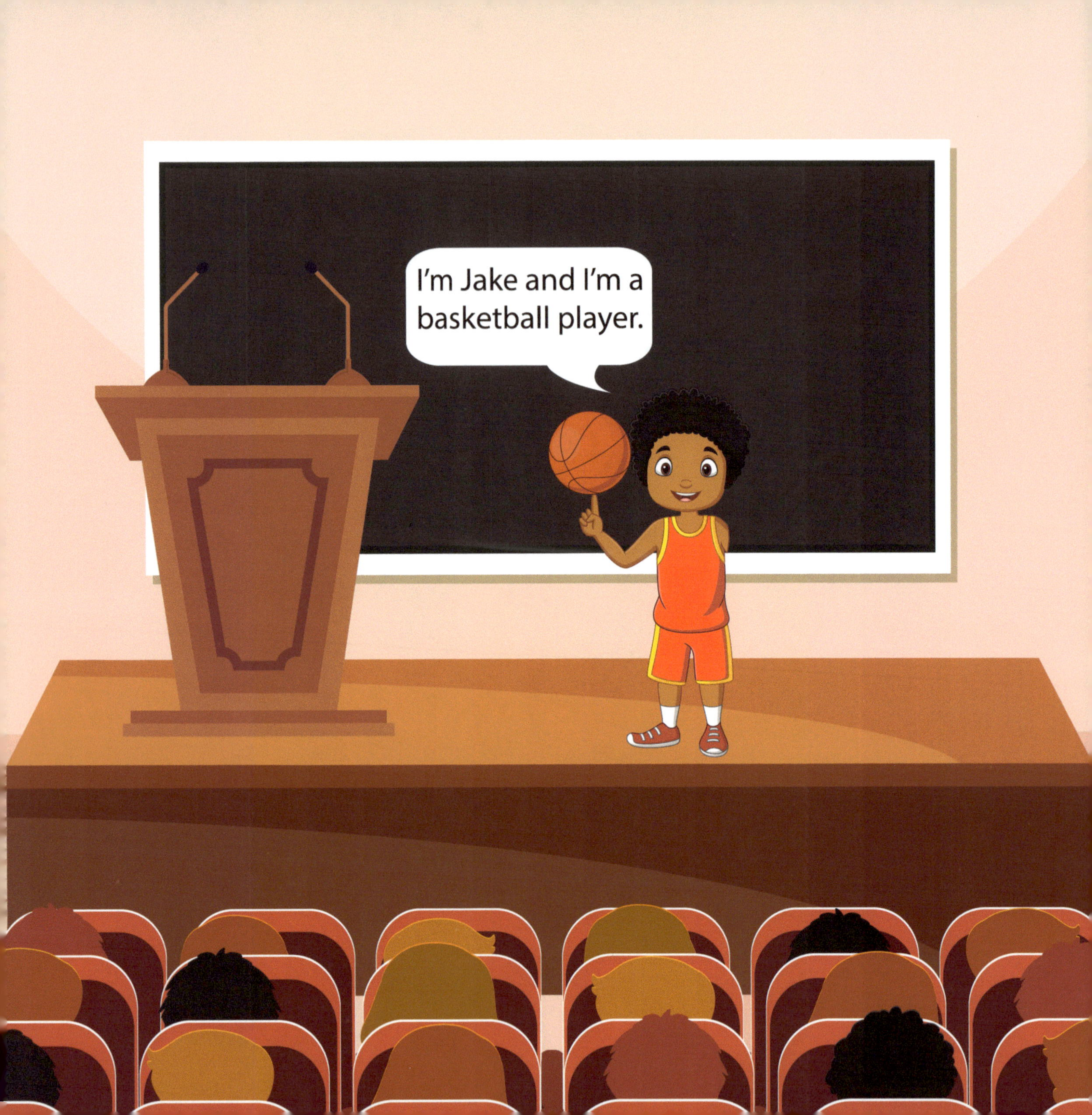
I'm Jake and I'm a basketball player.

The End!

www.ingramcontent.com/pod-product-compliance
Lightning Source LLC
Chambersburg PA
CBHW042119040426

42449CB00002B/103